MY FIRST BOOK

BULGARIA

ALL ABOUT BULGARIA FOR KIDS

GL●BED
CHILDREN BOOKS

Interior and cover Design: Daniel Day
Editor: Margaret Bam

For My Sons, Daniel, David and Jude

Rila Monastery, Bulgaria

Bulgaria

Bulgaria is a **country**.

A country is land that is controlled by a **single government**. Countries are also called **nations, states, or nation-states**.

Countries can be **different sizes**. Some countries are big and others are small.

Nessebar, Bulgaria

Where Is Bulgaria?

Bulgaria is located in the continent of Europe.

A continent is a massive area of land that is separated from others by water or other natural features.

Bulgaria is situated in the eastern part of Europe.

Sofia, Bulgaria

Capital

The capital of Bulgaria is Sofia.

Sofia is located in the **western part** of the country.

Sofia is the largest city in Bulgaria.

Veliko Tarnovo, Bulgaria

Provinces

Bulgaria is a country that is made up of 28 provinces.

The provinces of Bulgaria are as follows:

Blagoevgrad, Burgas, Dobrich, Gabrovo, Haskovo, Kardzhali, Kyustendil, Lovech, Montana, Pazardzh, Pernik, Pleven, Plovdiv, Razgrad, Ruse, Shumen, Silistra, Sliven, Smolyan, Sofia City, Sofia (province), Stara Zagora, Targovishte, Varna, Veliko Tarnovo, Vidin, Vratsa and Yambol.

Population

Bulgaria has population of around **6.8 million people** making it the 107th most populated country in the world and the 21st most populated country in Europe.

Melnik, Bulgaria

Size

Bulgaria is **110,879 square kilometres** making it the 16th largest country in Europe by area.

Bulgaria is the 105th largest country in the world.

Languages

The official language of Bulgaria is **Bulgarian**. The Bulgarian language originated in Bulgaria and is now spoken by millions of people across the world.

Sámi and Finnish are also spoken in Bulgaria.

Here are a few Bulgarian phrases
- **Как сте?** - How are you?
- **Добро утро** - Good morning
  DOBRO AUTRO

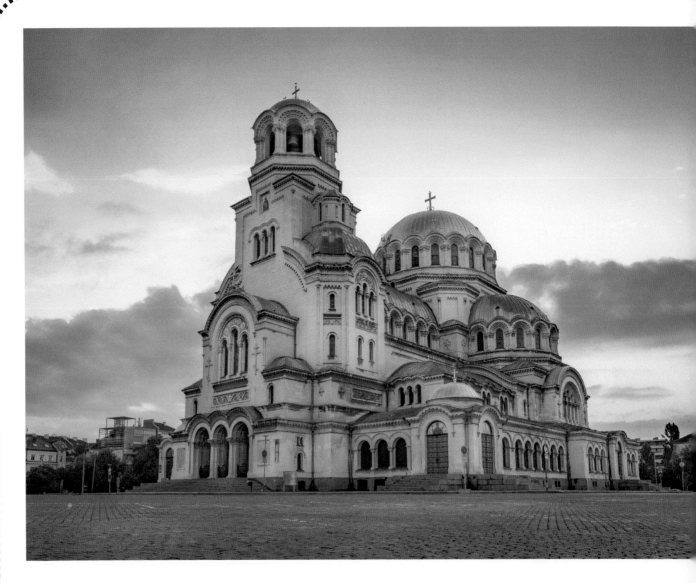

Alexander Nevasky Cathedral, Sofia, Bulgaria

Attractions

There are lots of interesting places to see in Bulgaria.

Some beautiful places to visit in Bulgaria are

- **Alexander Nevsky Cathedral**
- **Krushuna Waterfalls**
- **Koprivshtitsa**
- **Buzludzha Monument**

Byala, Bulgaria

History of Bulgaria

People have lived in Bulgaria for a very long time, in fact the earliest known human settlement in Bulgaria dates back to the Paleolithic era, and the area has been inhabited by Thracians, Greeks, Romans, and Byzantines throughout its history.

In 681 CE, the first Bulgarian state was founded, it became a major power in Europe during the reign of Khan Krum.

Bulgaria gained independence from the Ottoman Empire in 1878

People wearing traditional Folk Bulgarian costumes

Customs in Bulgaria

Bulgaria has many fascinating customs and traditions.

- On 6 January each year, Christian Bulgarians mark Jordan's Day. For Jordan's Day, it is customary for a priest to throw a cross into a river and all willing men jump after the cross in a competition to reach and retrieve it.

- A popular Bulgarian carnival is Kukeri (кукери). During this carnival, locals wear scary costumes and huge bells in order to drive away the evil spirits away.

Music of Bulgaria

There are many different music genres in Bulgaria such as **Bulgarian folk music, Jazz, Electronic and Rap.**

Some notable Bulgaria musicians include
- **Desi Slava**
- **Gloria**
- **Preslava**
- **Slavi Trifonov**
- **Azis**

Traditional Shopska Salad

Food of Bulgaria

Bulgaria is known for having delicious, flavoursome and rich dishes.

The national dish of Bulgaria is **Shopska** which is a cold salad traditionally made with chopped tomatoes and cucumbers.

Food of Bulgaria

Some popular dishes in Bulgaria include

- Tarator
- Meshana Skara
- Sarmi
- Shopska Salata
- Shkembe
- Kiselo Mlyako
- Moussaka

Sofia, Bulgaria

Weather in Bulgaria

Bulgaria has a diverse climate with significant regional variations due to its location in Southeast Europe. The country has a temperate continental climate with four distinct seasons.

In the summer months from June to August, the climate is generally hot and dry. While winters from December to February, are cold and snowy.

The warmest month in Bulgaria is August.

Dog in Bulgaria

Animals of Bulgaria

There are many wonderful animals in Bulgaria.

Here are some animals that live in Bulgaria

- Dalmatian pelican
- White stork
- European rabbit
- Egyptian vulture
- Red squirrel

Bulgarian mountains

Mountains

There are many beautiful mountains in Bulgaria which is one of the reasons why so many people visit this beautiful country every year.

Here are some of Bulgaria's mountains

- Vitosha
- Musala
- Vihren
- Botev Peak
- Golyam Perelik

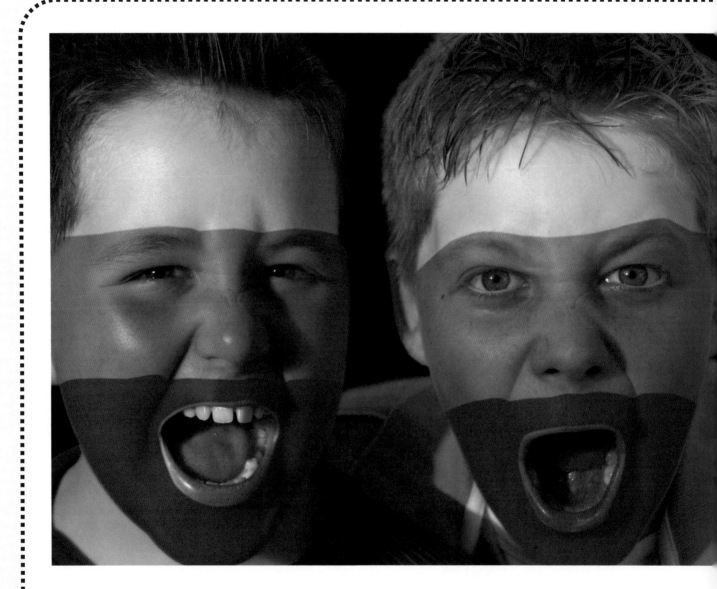

Bulgarian football fans

Sports of Bulgaria

Sports play an integral part in Bulgarian culture. The most popular sport is Football.

Here are some of famous sportspeople from Bulgaria

- Grigor Dimitrov - Tennis
- Vasil Etropolski - Fencing
- Yordan Bikov - Weightlifting
- Stefka Kostadinova - Athletics
- Kubrat Pulev - Boxing

Vasil Levski (1837-1873)

Famous

Many successful people hail from Bulgaria.

Here are some notable Bulgarian figures

- **Vasil Levski – Revolutionary**
- **Dimitar Berbatov – Footballer**
- **Maria Bakalova – Actress**
- **Grigor Dimitrov – Tennis Player**

Bulgarian flag

Something Extra...

As a little something extra, we are going to share some lesser known facts about Bulgaria.

- **The Bulgarian language is the oldest Slavic language still in use today.**
- **Bulgaria is the world's second-biggest exporter of rose oil.**
- **Bulgaria is home to some of the world's oldest gold artifacts, dating back over 6,000 years.**

Dalgopol, Bulgaria

Words From the Author

We hope that you enjoyed learning about the wonderful country of Bulgaria.

Bulgaria is a country rich in culture and beauty, with lots of wonderful places to visit and people to meet.

We hope you continue to learn more about this wonderful nation. If you enjoyed this book, consider leaving a review!

With Love

Printed in Great Britain
by Amazon